The
Cheviot Hills

By

Geoff Holland

First published in Great Britain in 2007 by Trailguides Limited.
www.trailguides.co.uk

ISBN 978-1-905444-17-5

Trailguides Limited
35 Carmel Road South
Darlington
Co Durham DL3 8DQ

The Cheviot: October

October stirs,
rises with the dawn,
climbs slowly across
your broad, brown back.

It is a silent day,
cool on this solemn hill,
peat pools
black as liquorice.

A cloud descends,
a cataract across
this drowsy hill.
Horizons disappear.

It is a quiet day,
high in Northumberland.
Time drifts,
soft as a whisper.

October bears me
no mischief.

CONTENTS

INTRODUCTION

1. The Cheviot Hills

The Cheviot Hills are England's most northerly hills and cover an area of some 400 square miles. They rise and fall along the northern edge of England, rolling down into Scotland in small, green, rounded waves. In the great scheme of matters mountainous, they are not especially big hills with the highest, The Cheviot, standing at a height of 2676 feet (815 metres). But with distant views to endless horizons and clouds billowing overhead, you cannot help but feel that this is truly big country.

The Cheviot Hills are volcanic in origin with deep, narrow valleys radiating from the central core. They are of national nature conservation importance, supporting extensive areas of blanket bog and heather moorland. They are remote and sparsely populated with vehicular access being restricted to the valley floors.

This is ideal walking territory where hours, even days, can pass without a chance meeting with another lonely wandering soul. In these wild, expansive hills the

The view towards Uswayford from The Middle. Walk 5 The Winding Road to Windy Gyle.

DNA of a long and fascinating past lies beneath every single footstep you take. As the wind sweeps across the seemingly endless curve of hills and through deep and remote valleys you will feel an unrivalled sense of isolation. Here the curlew is king and solitude is his queen.

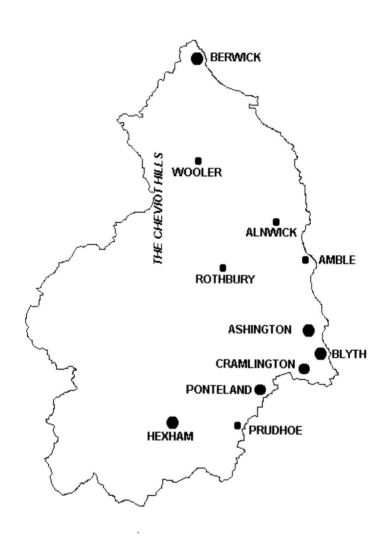

2. Access & the Right to Roam

Before 2005 a close examination of the Ordnance Survey map would have revealed that only two of the six summits in the Cheviot Hills exceeding 2000 feet in height were served by public rights of way. Whilst there were many public footpaths and bridleways criss-crossing the Cheviot Hills generally and a number of `permissive footpaths` had been negotiated with landowners, very few of the vast array of these hills enjoyed any public rights to their actual tops. The only exceptions, it seemed, were those hills crossed by the Pennine Way.

In practice, however, access to the hills was never a particular problem for those walkers and runners willing to ignore the definitive map. Perhaps this was down to the generally tolerant nature of Northumbrians!

Notwithstanding this situation `on the ground`, vast tracts of outstanding hill country, in an area forming part of the Northumberland National Park, were legally `off limits` to walkers, runners and similar outdoor enthusiasts. Thankfully, this wholly unsatisfactory position was consigned to history on the 28th May 2005 when the Countryside and Rights of Way Act 2000 finally became law.

"The Street" near Swineside Law . Walk 8 High Along The Border Line.

This landmark piece of legislation allows walkers and runners to roam freely on designated `access land` with no need to keep to official footpaths or bridleways. This new `access land` is now shown on the latest editions of the Ordnance Survey Explorer map (OL 16) marked with a light yellow coloured background and, at many entry points to the `access land`, stiles and gates carry the new `access land` waymarking symbol (a brown `stick` man in a brown circle).

The Act does, however, give landowners and farmers permission to restrict the 'right to roam' for up to 28 days each year. Also, some areas of the Cheviot Hills are managed grouse moors so it is important to be aware of the restrictions that may apply to walking with dogs. To find out more about the 'right to roam' and whether any general or specific restrictions apply to an area of the Cheviot Hills you intend to explore in the near future a visit to the website **www.countrysideaccess.gov.uk** will give you all the necessary information.

The Ministry of Defence owns a large area of the Cheviot Hills and uses much of this land for training purposes. A part of this area, known as the Otterburn Ranges, is used for live firing and, therefore understandably, recreational use of this particular area is severely restricted. You should not enter any part of this land when the 'red warning flags' are flying. None of the walks in this book use this restricted land although some walks do cross parts of the 'dry training area'. However, in this respect, there is absolutely no danger whatsoever and walkers should not feel intimidated or restricted in any way. For further information about the land ownership of the Ministry of Defence, visit **www.defence-estates.mod.uk**

3. The Walks

These walks, many of which take advantage of the 'right to roam' legislation, are intended to act as a broad introduction to the Cheviot Hills. They are not designed for absolute beginners as they require basic map reading and navigational skills. They are, in general, longer than the usual 'starter' walks and in many cases involve some fairly strenuous ascents. This said, the walks should be well within the capabilities of any reasonably fit walker, sensibly 'kitted out' for potentially changeable mountain weather. They also make excellent training circuits for those who prefer to run on the fells.

The walks have all been graded in accordance with the Ferguson Grading System ('FGS') and the actual grading is set out at the end of each individual walk. A detailed explanation of the FGS and how individual gradings are determined is set out on pages 57-59 in the Appendix to this book

In an age where the tentacles of the 'rules and regulations beast' seem to reach out in every conceivable direction, a day wandering in the hills offers an ideal means of escape. Experienced walkers and runners are usually pretty common-sense sort of folk with a desire to have a minimum impact on the countryside they hold so dear to their hearts. They know, for instance, to leave gates and property as they find them, to protect plants and animals, to take their litter home and to avoid starting fires. This is all pretty basic stuff. However, if you want to read more about the Countryside and Moorland Codes, before you

tackle any of the walks in this book, just log onto
www.countrysideaccess.gov.uk. It is all there in black and white.

These walks are also intended to give a flavour of 'what lies beneath the surface' and to offer a taste of the many facets which make these such wonderfully interesting hills. The route descriptions, which are easy to follow 'in the field' and contain Grid References at key points, should be used in conjunction with either of the two recommended maps.

4. The Weather

The prevailing south westerly wind sweeps in from the distant Atlantic Ocean shedding the majority of its precipitation before reaching the Cheviot Hills. The average annual rainfall on the high ground is 110 cm., less than half the rainfall of more popular mountain playgrounds such as the Lake District and the Scottish Highlands.

The driest months of the year tend to be March, April and June whilst the wettest are November, December and January. The latter part of August, the peak of the holiday season, is also often unsettled. During

Sheep stell in the mist.

January, February and March cold north winds can make walking on the high tops particularly demanding although a huge amount of snow is rare.

This said, walking in the Cheviot Hills can, at any time of the year, produce surprises. A cold, clear February day, an early morning frost and a blue, uncluttered sky can leave you with memories that will long outlive a day spent tramping the hills at the height of an English summer. It is all down to opportunities and personal preference.

5. The Maps

Two maps cover the Cheviot Hills: the Ordnance Survey Explorer (1: 25000) OL 16 and the Harvey Superwalker (1: 40000) The Cheviot Hills. Which one to choose is down to personal taste.

6. Towns, Villages & Accommodation

The town of Wooler, known as the 'Gateway to the Cheviots', is an ideal base for walkers wishing to explore the Cheviot Hills from the College, Harthope and Breamish Valleys, whilst Rothbury serves those bound for the hills of Upper Coquetdale. Both towns have a choice of accommodation, ranging from small hotels, guest houses, self catering cottages and caravan/camping sites, together with a selection of shops. In addition, there is a Youth Hostel in Wooler and bookings can be made online at **www.yha.org.uk** or by telephoning 01668281365. The villages of Powburn, Thropton, Harbottle and Alwinton, whilst generally closer to the hills, offer a more limited range of facilities. The Tourist Information Centres listed below will be able to assist you with your specific requirements.

7. Tourist Information Centres & Websites

The Northumberland National Park Authority (**www.northumberland-national-park.org.uk**) operate two Information Centres at Rothbury and Ingram, in the Breamish Valley. The address of the Rothbury National Park Centre is Church House, Church Street, Rothbury, NE65 7UP, telephone number 01669620887. It is only open at weekends between November and March. The address of the Ingram Visitor Centre is Ingram, Powburn, Alnwick, NE66 4LT, telephone number 01665578890. It is closed between November and March.

There is a Tourist Information Centre in Wooler at Cheviot Centre, 12 Padgepool Place, Wooler, Northumberland, NE71 6BL telephone number 01668 282123. It is open throughout the year.

Visitors to Wooler will find the website **www.wooler.org.uk** a useful source of information whereas visitors based in Rothbury should visit **www.visit-rothbury.co.uk**.

Above. Cushat Law from Great Standrop. Walk 1 The Ultimate Harthope Circuit.
Below. Akeld Hill "secondary summit". Walk 2 The Wandering Hills of Wooler.

Above. Rookland Sike. Walk 3 The Whitelands of Biddlestone.
Below. Climbing away from Alnhammoor Farm. Walk 4 The Alnhammoor Round.

Above. Heading towards Middle Hill. Walk 5 The Winding Road to Windy Gyle.
Below. From Yarnspath Law. Walk 6 High Circuit of the Usway Burn.

Above. Climbing away from Trowupburn. Walk 7 The Hethpool Border Circuit.
Below. The view from Swineside Law. Walk 8 High Along the Border Line.

14

WALK 1: THE ULTIMATE HARTHOPE CIRCUIT

The upper reaches of the Harthope Valley are dominated by the mighty Cheviot, on the north side, and the elegant Hedgehope Hill, on the south side. These, the two highest of the Cheviot Hills, are embedded into the subconscious of every self- respecting Northumbrian hill walker. An extended and unusual round of these must-climb hills, embracing the lesser tops of Great Standrop, High Cantle, Shielcleugh Edge, Coldlaw Cairn, Cairn Hill, Scald Hill and Blackseat Hill, takes you on a high level journey of discovery.

DISTANCE: 14.25 miles (22.9 km)
ASCENT: 3494 feet (1065 metres)
TERRAIN: Mixed fell with a variety of paths and tracks, many rough and boggy
TIME: 6.5 hours
START: Hawsen Burn, Harthope Valley (GR NT954225)

Grid References

Hawsen Burn	954 225
Step stile	956 213
Fence	946 194
Path	958 171
Rig Cairn	940 168
High Cantle	927 162
Cairn Hill	903 195
Track	934 225
Hawsen Burn	954 225

FGS Grading

Grading is F10 [D2, N2, T2, R2, H2]

THE WALK

1. Park on the roadside area of grass, close to the Hawsen Burn, the last point of public vehicular access in the Harthope Valley. A circular stone sheep stell, a common sight in the Cheviot Hills and so shaped to prevent snow drifting, stands next to the burn. On the other side of the single track road, a signpost points the way to Housey Crags and your first top of the day, Hedgehope Hill. A path alongside a dry stone wall, leads you to a tree shrouded wooden footbridge crossing the Harthope Burn. After you have made a quick climb through the trees, the impressive Housey Crags loom large in front of you. Over the step stile, and a steady lung testing climb up a clear, green path will soon bring you adjacent to and then behind these, the most frequently visited of all the North-umberland crags. Continue to follow the path, aided by an occasional directional fingerpost, across the splendid viewpoint of Long Crags and then to and over the next step stile **(GR NT956213).** Across the valley, the long, broad back of Northumberland's highest hill stretches out in the morning light. The path now bends towards the south west, as you wander across the cotton grass rich moor-land of Kelpie Strand in the direction of the `cone` of Hedgehope Hill. At the 450 metre contour, the path swings gently to your left, marking the start of a much steeper gradient, and a gain of over 260 metres in height in just over half a mile of walking. The 714 metre high, cairn capped summit of Hedgehope Hill will come as something of a relief as tears of sweat begin to slip from your brow. A trig point sits snugly inside the large grey stone cairn, which also pro-vides shelter from the rarely absent wind.

2. After reaching this point in 1898, Edmund Bogg wrote in his book, `A Thou-sand Miles of Wandering in the Border Country`, ".....we assembled on the loose cairn after a quick ascent and lingered to enjoy the view", adding, "Hedgehope is markedly conical in shape and stands out boldly from the general mass of Cheviot for which it is sometimes mistaken". Having similarly lingered examining every angle of the fine view, it is now time for you to cross the step stile and to descend in a south easterly direction, with the post and wire fence on your left. After first crossing relatively level ground, with Threestoneburn Wood stretching away to the east, the hill drops sharply downhill before reaching a fence **(GR NT946194)** heading in a south westerly direction towards Standrop Rigg. This is your route, best taken along the opposite side of the fence, and as you make your way steadily downhill the granite tors of Great and Little Stan-drop begin to grow in stature. Tors such as these, which are similar to those found on the granite outcrops of south west England, are especially rare in the Cheviot Hills. As you pass Little Standrop, a diversion away from the fence on a path cutting diagonally to your left, to climb the twin topped Great Standrop, is

16

an absolute must. The views are outstanding in all directions. Back with the fence and, after a further steep downhill stretch of just under half a mile, best walked on the opposite side of the fence, you will arrive at the point where the Coldlaw and Standrop Burns converge to form the Linhope Burn. This is a peaceful spot.

3. You must now turn left and follow the gravel track as it makes its way above the north bank of the charming burn passing en route a `log cabin`. After just under one mile of pleasant walking, the Het Burn tumbles down the hillside on your left, immediately before the track meets the main, signposted path to Hedgehope Hill. The bare remains of a Bronze Age settlement are scattered across this area, including five hut circles, surrounded by a wider field system. Earlier excavations uncovered a stone hearth and several fragments of pottery. Continue across the gated, wooden bridge and, on reaching the opposite bank of the burn, continue with the track as far as the first bend to the right. At this point, leave the track behind by turning to your left and heading in the direction of a large and obvious rowan tree. Once beyond the tree you will join a path running from right to left. Turn left and on reaching the steep drop **(GR NT958171)** to the base of the waterfall, take care following the thin path downwards. This is Linhope Spout, certainly the most visited of all of the Cheviot waterfalls and possibly the most impressive, especially after heavy rain or during rapidly melting snow. The normally slim waterfall, which cascades a distance of 56 feet, certainly impressed writer Agnes Herbert when she visited here in 1923. In her book, `Northumberland`, she wrote "......the booming of the cataract came to our ears before we reached Linhope and suddenly, without warning, the torrent flashed into sight". With more than a hint of poetic licence, she continued to wax lyrical, saying "....the water fell down the precipitous sides of pointed rocks in exceeding volume, and then broke up, descending quite slowly, like snow". Judge for yourself and enjoy a moment of relaxation before heading, once again, for higher ground.

4. Climb back up the thin path and, as the path broadens, continue to your left towards and past a signpost. On reaching a second signpost, alongside a five bar gate and a more intimate `kissing gate`, pass through and turn immediately right to follow the fence as far as the gravel track. Continue straight across in the direction of a five bar gate and soon you will join a green track. The remains of a small Bronze Age settlement stand nearby and include two hut circles. The remnants of two Roman period settlements also lie nearby, one containing two hut circles arranged around a small sunken yard and the other surrounded by a circular enclosure. Go through the gate and continue along the track, with Ritto Hill to your left, and as you gain a little height the impressive flanks of Shill Moor come into view slightly to your left. When the track begins its gentle descent and decides to split in two be sure to head for the left hand five bar gate. Once through, take the right hand spur to start a long, gradual climb uphill on a clear, sometimes boggy, quad track. Eventually you will pass the height of Rig Cairn (**GR NT940168**) topped with a small walkers cairn. This makes a perfect place to 'take a breather' and to enjoy the extensive views. Not far from this spot, on the 24th/25th March 1943, a Junkers Ju 88 aircraft crashed killing all four crew. Continue with the track over fairly boggy ground and, in time, you will reach a five bar gate in a post and wire fence.

5. This fence runs across the high ground between High Cantle and Coldlaw Cairn and, once across, walk straight ahead to pick up a quad track. Turn right and head for the 482 metre high summit of High Cantle, marked with a tiny cairn **(GR NT927162)**. To the south west lies the pencil straight River Breamish, watched over by three powerful looking hills, Bloodybush Edge, Cushat Law and Shill Moor. Return to the fence by making a north easterly 'bee line' and, turning left, continue over rough and boggy ground, crossing the indiscernible top of Shielcleugh Edge en route to the rocky Coldlaw Cairn. Stay with the fence all of the way. This is one of the loneliest and elemental heights in these weather beaten hills. You are literally miles from anywhere, with the vast swathe of the Uswayford Forest away to the south west and the dominating presence of the mighty Cheviot to the north. You are 9 miles into your journey and you will feel utterly alone. Savour the moment. Keeping with the fence, continue in the direction of Comb Fell, the third highest of the Cheviot Hills, until you reach another fence climbing up from the Harthope Valley to your left. Go over the step stile, turn immediately left and follow the fence towards the head of the valley and whilst the going is generally easy, there are two substantial peat hags to negotiate along the way, so be prepared to get your hands a little dirty. Soon you begin to rise again as you cross the watershed of the Harthope Burn, an area named on the Ordnance Survey map as Scotsman's Knowe. The word 'knowe' means 'the rounded top or shoulder of a hill'.

6. When you reach the directional fingerpost, take a deep breath and, keeping the fence to your left, begin the steep climb towards the top of Cairn Hill **(GR NT903195)**, the south western outhill of The Cheviot. At 777 metres high, Scotsman's Cairn is an excellent viewpoint, as wave after wave of hills roll away to the south. Across the valley the peat hag fringed ridge between Hedgehope Hill and Comb Fell dominates the view Once across the step stile, the signpost points to the west and the Pennine Way. Your route turns to the right. An earlier visitor to these heights, Stephen Oliver, warned in his 1835 book 'Rambles in Northumberland', "…..as Cheviot is frequently enveloped in a sudden mist, a stranger ought never to venture on to it alone" adding "..its top is a perfect bog, in some places quite impassable from the accumulation of water". No such problem for a 21st century traveller, as you make your way along the mill-stone pathway past a small lough on the opposite side of the fence, to the mono-lithic trig point on the summit of this 815 metre high hill. Local shepherds used to meet near to the summit of The Cheviot in July and November each year to ex-change sheep that had strayed from one area to another. These long established meetings, which were known as `Cheviot Gatherings`, came to an end in the late 1950's and stray sheep are now exchanged by road. Such is the unstoppable march of progress!

7. Stay with the stone pathway, as it continues across the summit plateau in a north easterly direction, cross over the ladder stile and then start your descent, now with the fence to your left, towards Scald Hill. Heading steeply downwards, you will enjoy fine views to the Harthope Valley and beyond to the Northumber-land coast. Immediately after a short, invariably boggy, col a quick and easy climb delivers you to the top of the 549 metre high Scald Hill. To your left, the remote Lambden Valley is just visible. Continue downhill and when, after a short while, the fence turns to the north, be sure to keep the fence company. Eventually, you will encounter a short, sharp drop to the watershed of the New Burn. As you clamber towards the top of the opposite side of this deep cut in the hillside, you will see to your right a rough track cutting a way through the shin deep heather **(GR NT934225).**

8. This is your easterly route to the craggy top of the 461 metre high Blackseat Hill. Standing beside the small cairn on the rocky summit, you will enjoy excel-lent views of the Harthope Valley and its fine collection of crags, to the north east, and of The Cheviot, to the south west. Now it is time to descend back to the Harthope Valley and, continuing in a generally easterly direction, a faint path very briefly leads the way off the crag topped summit. Just short of the heather line this comes to an abrupt end. Turn left and in due course you will meet up with a splendidly green track which heads all the way back to the valley, crossing the New Burn en route. Once the tarmac road is reached, turn left and soon you will be back beside the Hawsen Burn in one of Northumberland's most beautiful valleys.

Cushat Law from High Cantle.

FGS Grading

Grading is F10 [D2, N2, T2, R2, H2]

Distance	2	12 – 18 miles
Navigation	2	Competent navigation skills needed
Terrain	2	25 -50% on graded track or path 50 – 75% off / single track
Remoteness	2	Countryside not in close proximity to habitation – less than 20% of the route within 2 miles
Height	2	Over 125 ft per mile

WALK 2: THE WANDERING HILLS OF WOOLER

The attractive, stone built town of Wooler lies at the north eastern corner of the
Cheviot Hills. To the west, a delightful line of small, rounded hills, scattered with
the remnants of a distant past, clamber up from the green plain below. To the
south of the windswept summits, heather moors stretch out towards the heart of
these wild northern hills. This walk allows you to dip your toes in the waters of
the total Cheviot experience as you wander out across the wide open spaces along
the extreme edge of the Northumberland National Park.

DISTANCE: 10 miles (16.1 km)
ASCENT: 1903 feet (580 metres)
TERRAIN: Mainly good green tracks and paths with some gravel tracks
TIME: 4.5 hours
START: Humbleton Burn Picnic Area (GR NT976272)

Grid References

Humbleton Burn picnic area	976 272
Gate	961 259
Signpost	946 253
Uphill track	930 268
Path junction	927 282
250 metre contour	943 292
Path bend	959 289
Green track	967 287
Gate	974 279
Humbleton Burn picnic area	976 272

FGS Grading

Grading is F9 [D1, N2, T2, R2, H2]

THE WALK

1. Leave the centre of Wooler, via Ramsey's Lane, and park at the Humbleton Burn Picnic Area below the tree covered slopes of Kenterdale Hill and Brown's Law. Sandwiches packed and it is time to follow the path, signposted 'Wooler Common ¾ Broadstruther 3', which leaves the tarmac road just prior to the bridge across the Humbleton Burn. Keep with the thin path as it first follows the burn. Once past the five bar gate, the path begins to climb uphill, turning eventually westwards towards Wooler Common Farm. On reaching the signpost, follow the public footpath which passes to the right of the buildings, and, once past, cross over two step stiles in quick succession, turning right after the second one to follow a gravel track past a plantation on your left. Soon you will reach open moorland, with superb views of the whale backed Cheviot, with Braydon Crag particularly prominent. The curved beaked curlew, emblem of the Northumberland National Park, breeds on these upland moors and to hear its distinctive call is to discover just a small piece of the Cheviot jigsaw. Continue straight ahead and on reaching a directional fingerpost take the subsidiary green track to the left. Within 200 metres you will pass through a small gate **(GR NT961259)** and then begins your descent of the delightful Hellpath.

2. This path cuts diagonally across the lower slopes of the crag topped Watch Hill, an important lookout post during the 15th and 16th century border troubles. You are also on the route of the annual 20 mile long Chevy Chase Fell Race, an event which was first held in 1955 as the Chevy Chase Walk, with rucksacks and boots then being worn by all competitors. The name derives from the old border ballad, 'Chevy Chase', which tells the tale of the 1388 Battle of Otterburn between the troops of Earl Percy of Northumberland and Earl Douglas of Scotland. To your left, the 'glidders' of the steep sided Hart Heugh tumble down to the Carey Burn as it flows towards the Harthope Burn. On reaching the bottom of the hill and a directional fingerpost, the path bends to the right and follows the water's edge as far as the wooden footbridge. Here, just beyond the point where the Common Burn, to the right, joins the Broadstruther Burn, on the left, the Carey Burn begins its short, but lively, life. Once across the bridge, the path climbs for a short distance before levelling out and heading westwards. The going, initially through broom and bracken and then patches of heather, is easy as the view ahead to Broadstruther, once a remote farmstead but now used as a shelter for use by shooting parties, opens up.

3. Where the path splits in two beside a directional fingerpost **(GR NT946253)**, take the right hand fork climbing uphill in a north westerly direction along a good, green track. Continue with the path as it crosses almost a mile of wide open grass and heather moor towards the remote dwelling of Commonburn House, with the unnamed and fairly impressive crags to your right. If you are tempted, as surely you will, to explore these crags as a small deviation from the main route, you will come upon a track, to your right, which will lead you most of the way. The extra effort is certainly worthwhile. The occasional directional fingerpost will keep you on the 'straight and narrow' as the track diminishes in width. As you begin to come near to the building you will need to cross the Common Burn via a shallow ford and head to the right hand side of the very neat and well maintained house. Just beyond the house, after passing through a five bar gate, turn right along a gravel track and, after crossing a cattle grid, then turn left along an uphill track **(GR NT930268)**. Now follows a relatively easy walk of just less then 1 mile as you head, with Newton Tors rising away to your left and the distinctive Yeavering Bell straight ahead, towards a brief encounter with the 62½ mile long St. Cuthbert's Way. As you go, be sure to take the left hand fork, when the track splits in two, and, slightly further on, to continue straight ahead after climbing over a ladder stile.

4. Eventually, you will reach the cairn marked junction with the 1996 inaugurated St. Cuthbert's Way **(GR NT927282)**, a footpath which links together the religious sites of Melrose Abbey and Lindisfarne. Here you must turn sharp right, as indicated by a directional fingerpost, and follow St. Cuthbert's Way as far as the next ladder stile, some 600 metres south eastwards. On reaching the stile, which you do not cross, bid farewell to the Celtic cross waymarked track by turning left and heading uphill, with the stone wall firmly to your right. Before you have time to catch your breath, you will reach, slightly to the left of the wall you have been following for some 200 metres, the rocky promontory of Tom Tallon's Crag standing at 353 metres and, surprisingly, the highest point of the walk. The views from this quiet spot are expansive and with almost 6 miles now under your belt, it is a perfect place to 'tuck into your bait'. On leaving the crag, keep to the left of the dry stone wall and a ¾ mile downhill walk brings you to a tiny col. From here, a short, sharp climb leads quickly to the summit of the 302 metre high White Law. After again enjoying the extensive views, particularly to the Iron Age hillfort topped Yeavering Bell, cross over the vertigo inducing ladder stile and continue steeply downhill, the wall now to your left. As you close in on the 250 metre contour **(GR NT943292)** and some 50 metres short of a small gate on your left, turn to your right and head along a thin trace towards the 254 metre top of Akeld Hill. Once reached, be sure to then cut across the col, to the east, to reach the cairn crowned subsidiary top, lower by a mere 13 metres, but with an outstanding panorama across Milfield Plain. Situated at the base of the hill is the ancient hamlet of Akeld which, over 700 years ago, was a prosperous and wealthy settlement consisting of 13 households.

5. Return to the col and begin your descent by heading to Glead's Cleugh and then turning to your left down a clear green quad track to reach a good gravel track. This heads downhill to the buildings of Gleadscleugh. Do not take this track, instead cut straight across to join a subsidiary and parallel track which leads you downhill and, in turn, across the culverted Akeld Burn. This then leads you to the lower slopes of Harehope Hill where you will follow the field boundary, on your left, as it heads south eastwards before turning to the north east. There is a clear path to follow. When the path turns to the east **(GR NT959289),** you will pass the remains of an early Iron Age defended settlement, consisting of an enclosure contained within banks of earth and stone, which enjoys fantastic views back towards Akeld Hill and across Milfield Plain. Keep with the path as it passes through two small gates, both with adjoining ladder stiles, as far as the rocky gap at the bottom of the slopes of Humbleton Hill. At this point, turn right onto a green track **(GR NT967287)** which heads in a south westwards direction along the north western base of Humbleton Hill. Keep with this rising track until you reach a directional fingerpost and a step stile slightly to your left, which leads you to the final climb towards the summit of Humbleton Hill along the upper edge of a dry, stone scattered melt water channel. Nearby, on the 14th September 1402, the famous and exceedingly bloody Battle of Homildon Hill took place.

6. On reaching the large summit cairn you will have excellent views of Wooler. As you stand here, inevitably with the wind in your hair, it is easy to understand why our Iron Age ancestors chose to build a hillfort on this 298 metre high hill. Built in about 300 BC, the hillfort was one of the most strongly defended forts in the area. Leave the hill by heading in a south easterly direction, cutting through a gap in the stone ramparts, to pick up a green path which descends, in time, to a five bar gate **(GR NT974279),** leading onto a fence lined track. Turn right and, once again, head uphill. After passing through a five bar gate, be sure to take the track which heads off to the left and which, after first crossing open ground, cuts through a small plantation leading you back to your patiently waiting car at the Humbleton Burn Picnic Area, via a wooden footbridge across the burn. When you eventually wind your way home through the sleepy town of Wooler, it is worth remembering the words of a certain Eneas Mackenzie, who, in his 1825 book `An Historical View of the County of Northumberland` advised his readers that, "there are several inns in Wooler, some of which are respectable, particularly the Black Bull Inn". By 1926, William Ford Robertson in his book `Walks from Wooler`, was able to helpfully add that, "here in one respect we are able to say that the town has improved, for the compliment is now certainly no less deserved by all the others". As more than 80 years have now `passed under the bridge`, and more than likely thirsty after a satisfying day in the hills, you may just be tempted to carry out your own small piece of 'market research'.

The unnamed crags en-route to Commonburn House.

FGS Grading

Grading is F9 [D1, N2, T2, R2, H2]

Distance	1	6 – 12 miles
Navigation	2	Competent navigation skills needed
Terrain	2	25 -50% on graded track or path 50 – 75% off / single track
Remoteness	2	Countryside not in close proximity to habitation – less than 20% of the route within 2 miles
Height	2	Over 125 ft per mile

WALK 3: THE WHITELANDS OF BIDDLESTONE

The history soaked settlement of Biddlestone stands on the southern edge of the Cheviot Hills. To the north, a succession of grass covered hills climb up towards the vast Kidland Forest and the lonely summit of Wether Cairn. To the south, the Vale of Whittingham stretches out towards the sombre backcloth of the Simonside Hills. Trickling sikes, rushing burns, deep cleughs and steep sided valleys characterise this switchback walk of wall to wall panoramas. It is a wide screen, cinematic journey.

DISTANCE: 8.5 miles (13.7 km)
ASCENT: 1936 feet (590 metres)
TERRAIN: Mixed grassland with a number of good green tracks/paths. Some pathless terrain and short stretches of tarmac and gravel.
TIME: 4.5 hours
START: Alongside road to Clennell Hall, Alwinton (GR NT925062)

Grid References

Roadside	925 062
Wall corner	927 073
Gates	943 092
Gate	942 100
Fence	943 113
Gate	939 105
Animal feed store	925 097
Roadside	925 062

FGS Grading

Grading is F9 [D1, N2, T2, R2, H2]

THE WALK

1. Immediately before reaching the Upper Coquetdale village of Alwinton, turn right along the single track road, signposted Clennell Hall. Park on the grass haugh **(GR NT925062)** prior to the bridge across the River Alwin. Now your journey continues on foot, following the road which hugs the river bank and soon passing Clennell Hall, now an hotel and a riverside holiday park. First referred to in 1242, it is believed that the `deserted` medieval village of Clennell, one of the `Ten Towns of Coquetdale`, was cleared to make way for the park and garden surrounding Clennell Hall. The hall, which is a Grade II Listed Building, occupies a strategic position at the entrance to the valley and consists of a medieval tower house and an attached 17th century house with 18th and 19^{h} century additions. Keeping alongside the river, you will pass a small footbridge, on your left, before crossing over a cattle grid. After some 400 metres, at the corner of the dry stone wall **(GR NT927073),** leave the main valley track to your right and follow the gravel track which angles uphill towards the corner of a plantation. Go through the five bar gate and head diagonally across the lush, green field, passing to the right of a tiny square plantation. You are aiming for the bottom right hand corner of the next plantation, where you will cross a small step stile over a post and wire fence. There are pleasant views back over towards Upper Coquetdale. With the trees to your left, continue uphill towards the small gate at the extreme edge of the same plantation. Go through the gate and, almost immediately, a second gate. The clear path ahead climbs towards the saddle between Clennell and Silverton Hills.

2. On reaching the saddle, the 322 metre high summit of Clennell Hill lies a short distance to your left and is a mere 12 metres higher than the ground on which you are standing. You might just be tempted to make the short journey to claim an unscheduled `top`. It would be a shame not to. To the south west of the summit, at the end of a high spur, lie the remains of the Iron Age hillfort of Camp Knowe. The hillfort measures 96 metres by 80 metres and is enclosed by a large rampart of earth and stone. Now cut through the small gate in the fence and, on a clear path, start your steep descent to the skinny valley of Rookland Sike. As the bottom of the hill approaches, cross the step stile, next to a small gate, before splashing through the thin trickle of water. After crossing another step stile, climb towards the ruined buildings of Old Rookland, above you and slightly to your right. This derelict farm, with its three distinctive trees, was once the home of John Dagg, who left here together with his family of 4 children in May 1939 for a life as a shepherd at the now whitewashed cottage of Dunsdale in the Lambden Valley. In December 1944, John, his dog Sheila and a fellow shepherd rescued 4 members of the crew of a bomb laden U.S. Army Air Force B17 Flying Fortress aircraft which had crashed into Braydon Crag, north west of The Cheviot summit. As a result of their actions the shepherds received the British Empire Medal and border collie Sheila received the Dickin Medal, the animal equivalent of the Victoria Cross. Pass through the facing five bar gate and keep to the left of the buildings. Once you are beyond the sad and lonely ruins, turn right and head in a north easterly direction on a clear green track, keeping parallel with the fence. After half a mile of easy walking you will reach a red gravel track which leads ultimately to the secluded farm of Puncherton. Go through the two gates **(GR NT943092).**

3. After the second gate, turn left to follow the post and wire fence for a further 250 metres. At this point, leave the fence and, turning to your right, walk the short distance to the 412 metre high top of Gills Law. From here there are fine views to the well manicured green surrounds of Puncherton farm. Now head across the flat top of the hill, in a north westerly direction, following an excellent green track most of the 600 metres or so to the next step stile, standing alongside a small gate **(GR NT942100).** Once across, turn to your right and head downhill, in a north easterly direction, following the virtually pathless route of the public bridleway towards the circular sheep stell. Just after here, the bridleway crosses a fence and then contours the southern slopes of Bleak Law. This is not your route. Instead you must keep to the western side of the fence, heading uphill. These areas of grassland are known locally as `whitelands` because the erect spikes that are produced by the grass in June become bleached to almost white as autumn approaches. In his 1895 book, `Whittingham Vale, Northumberland: Its History, Traditions and Folklore`, David `Dippie` Dixon wrote of these hills "Delightful it is in summer time with a clear bright sky overhead, to wander over those breezy uplands". And so it is, at any time of the year! There is now a steady climb of one mile to the summit of Wether Cairn as you stay within shouting distance of the fence. As you gain height you will pick up a helpful track, which eases the going, a little!

4. The Kidland Forest now pops its head above the brow of the hill and you are on your way to a height gain of nearly 200 metres, eventually meeting up with another fence **(GR NT943113),** arriving from St. David's Cairn. On the 17th February 1945, little more than 200 metres to the east of this spot, a Halifax bomber crashed killing all but one of its seven man crew. Due to poor visibility, the aircraft had aborted its bombing mission to North West Germany and, as its home base of RAF Tholthorp, near York, was fog bound, the aircraft was diverted to RAF Winfield, close to Berwick. The sole survivor was found the following day injured and staggering around the hillside in thick mist. All but one of the crew were aged 24 or less. Turn left and, on reaching the next fence, cross over the step stile and put your boots straight into shin deep heather. The summit of Wether Cairn is now within sight, as first you pass a small shelter cairn and then arrive at the trig point adorned top. At 563 metres high, this is a decent sized hill but, with flat heather moorland stretching away to the north, there is little sense of height in that direction. The conical, cairn crowned Hogdon Law lies less than one mile away to the north east, whilst Cushat Law, Bloodybush Edge, Dunmoor Hill, Hedgehope Hill, The Cheviot and Windy Gyle crowd the more distant horizon. The broad sweep of the Kidland Forest lies to the west.

5. Time to turn tail and to head back to the step stile and once on the other side turn right. After 200 metres, adjacent to a step stile and an adjoining gate, bid `au revoir` to the fence and strike out on a 200° magnetic bearing across initially rough ground. After a further 400 metres you will see, slightly right of centre, the steep grass slopes tumbling down to the Allerhope Burn and, on the other side of the narrow valley, the edge of the Kidland Forest. You are aiming for Puncherton Hill but, initially, you need to set your sights to the left of the steep slopes and a distant five bar gate **(GR NT939105).** You will find the line which suits you best as you saunter carefree over the expansive grasslands. Once through the gate keep on a 240° magnetic bearing, utilising from time to time a green track. At the next fence, go through the five bar gate, turn left, go through a second gate and then turn right to follow the post and wire fence to the top of Puncherton Hill. From this 410 metre high hill you can peer down to the secluded Allerhope Burn, on the edge of the Kidland Forest, and the impressive Ravens Crag. The forest is one of the last strongholds of the endangered red squirrel.

6. Leave the top of the hill by staying with the track and, after passing through a five bar gate, you will begin to turn towards the south west as you descend in the direction of a corrugated animal feed store **(GR NT925097).** Crossing a slight depression, above White Slack, your route bends to the south as you start the gentle climb to the top of The Dodd. Standing at a height of 332 metres, this hill offers fantastic views down to the valley of the River Alwin, so be sure to spend some time to explore the western edges of the summit area. Continue to head south, eyes firmly set on another corrugated animal feed store, and follow the clear, steep path down the `nose` of The Dodd. Once at the bottom, you are now in the valley of the River Alwin with the Puncherton Burn rushing downhill on your left. Turn left and follow the red track twisting and turning down the valley, flanked by steep sided hills. Particularly outstanding are the scree shattered slopes of Clennell Hill, rising sharply away to your left, immediately after the cattle grid and the first bridge. The River Alwin is one of the many tributaries of the River Coquet, a river designated a Site of Special Scientific Interest (SSSI) under the Wildlife and Countryside Act 1981. The River Alwin, which is also included in the SSSI, is an extensive sea trout spawning ground. Continue with the river and enjoy a delightful 1½ mile stroll back to your starting point. If it is your lucky day you might just catch sight of a grey heron as it waits motionless, ready to catch its lunch.

Wether Cairn summit.

FGS Grading

Grading is F9 [D1, N2, T2, R2, H2]

Distance	1	6 – 12 miles
Navigation	2	Competent navigation skills needed
Terrain	2	25 -50% on graded track or path 50 – 75% off / single track
Remoteness	2	Countryside not in close proximity to habitation – less than 20% of the route within 2 miles
Height	2	Over 125 ft per mile

WALK 4: THE ALNHAMMOOR ROUND

The lower stretches of the valley of the River Breamish, more often referred to as the Ingram Valley, have been popular with generations of day-trippers and pic-nickers. The rolling, sun bleached hills to the south rise up from the valley to-wards the ancient Salter's Road, which climbs from the settlement of Alnham, crosses the slopes of Shill Moor and descends into the Upper Breamish Valley. This walk introduces you to this south east corner of the Cheviot Hills, offering wide angle views across time swept landscapes. The final climb, to the summit of Shill Moor, is the `piece de résistance`.

DISTANCE: 9.5 miles (15.3 km)
ASCENT: 1,608 feet (490 metres)
TERRAIN: Mixed fell, mainly good tracks (some gravel), paths and stretches of tarmac.
TIME: 5 hours
START: Near Hartside Farm (GR NT978162)

Grid References

Near Hartside Farm	978 162
Plantation corner	978 142
Sheep stell	982 138
Track junction	984 120
Gate	971 130
Road	964 133
Signpost	950 142
Track/Salter's Road junction	946 144
Shill Moor	946 154
Near Hartside Farm	978 162

FGS Grading

Grading is F9 [D1, N2, T2, R2, H2]

THE WALK

1. There is adequate verge parking immediately prior to the farm of Hartside, the last point of public vehicular access along the single track road. The tarmac continues as far as the hamlet of Linhope from where a track climbs to Linhope Spout, arguably the most impressive of the Cheviot waterfalls. However, your route begins by turning left before the farm, following the signposted road to Alnhammoor. Within half a mile the road crosses the River Beamish over a bailey bridge which was built in 1952 to replace a ford and a nearby footbridge. Just before the farm buildings turn left, at the roadside directional fingerpost, go over the step stile, cut straight across the field and exit through a small gate. Turn slightly to your left and head downhill to cross the Shank Burn via a small bridge and, after passing through a five bar gate, cut across the field on a good green track. Just prior to reaching the next five bar gate, take the track which heads uphill, to your right, cross over the next step stile and continue climbing on a rather 'churned up' track. Soon you will pass a circular sheep stell, on your left, and then an old wind bent rowan tree. The rowan tree, also known as the mountain ash, features prominently in Greek mythology. The goddess of youth, Hebe, dispensed rejuvenating ambrosia to the gods from her magic chalice. When she carelessly lost this chalice to demons, the gods sent an eagle to recover it and the feathers and drops of blood, which the eagle shed in the ensuing fight, where each turned into a rowan tree. The tree derived the shape of its leaves from the eagle's feathers and the appearance of its berries from the drops of blood. Before you leave the tree behind be sure to take in the view of Hedgehope, Dunmoor and Ritto Hills which has opened up behind you.

2. Continue to climb towards the right hand corner of the plantation (**GR NT978142**), where the track then dips down and fords the Cobden Burn. As you step over the stile, beside the gate, a few grass covered mounds to your left are all that remain of the hillside cottage of Cobden. Slightly to your right, alongside Cobden Sike, lie the remains of a large burial cairn with a smaller, earlier cairn buried inside. This indicates that the cairn was used over a long period of time, most likely during the Bronze Age. Keep with the main deeply cut track and then, after 200 metres, cut diagonally to your right to pick up, after a further 75 metres, a reasonably good green track. Stride onwards and soon you will pass a circular sheep stell, downhill to your left (**GR NT982138**), as the track begins to fade to a thin path and then peters out altogether. At this point, where there are vague signs of an old fence line, you will need to be eagle eyed. Watch out for the directional fingerpost, some 50 metres to your left, standing on a small green island in a pool of muddy water. Follow the arrow which points in a southerly direction and soon your path bends to the left and, within a matter of minutes, meets a red gravel track. Now for some straight forward walking as you turn right, to follow the track towards the next five bar gate. Pass through the gate and, with the flat top of the Simonside Hills now clearly in view, continue for a further 600 metres, to the point where the road makes a 90° turn to the right. Decision time! Do you want to claim the unscheduled top of the 341 metre high Hart Law, a delightfully green hill which enjoys tremendous views across the Vale of Whittingham and a fantastic panorama of the Cheviot heartland. If so, the just under one mile return journey starts by turning left and heading uphill towards the small plantation. Once you have gained a little height you will see the trig point topped summit a short 'bee line' away. Return along the same 'bee line'.

3. Continue with the red gravel track and very quickly you will arrive at a track junction (**GR NT984120**), marked with a directional fingerpost, where you will need to turn sharp right. You are now on the course of the Salter's Road, heading in a north westerly direction, along part of a medieval route used by traders carrying their goods from the North Sea coast saltpans across the border into Scotland. The route was also used by smugglers and thieves and, at one time, the road was known as the 'Thieves Road'. You are also standing slightly to the north east of the 320 metre high summit of Northfieldhead Hill and the remains of an Iron Age settlement. The near circular site is surrounded by a turf covered earth bank and traces of at least 15 round houses have been found here. Outside the site there is evidence of early farming. You will now stay with the Salter's Road for the next 3 miles, as first you ford a burn and then rise gently to reach a metal gate and a ladder stile. This is 'White Gate', named, not, as you will discover, because of the colour of the actual gate, but probably as a consequence of this being the entrance to an area of bleached grasslands, known locally as 'whitelands'. Follow the right hand directional arrow and stride out across the wide open grasslands in a north westerly direction, with the prominent cone of Hogdon Law, to your left, and Dunmoor Hill, to your right. You will contour High Knowes, on a clear track, passing through a gate (**GR NT971130**) as you head towards and then alongside the right hand edge of a plantation. When a gate is reached, pass through, and make the short descent to the road (**GR NT964133**) leading from the settlement of Alnham to the remote farmstead of Ewartly Shank, once called Shank House.

4. In his 1895 book, 'Whittingham Vale, Northumberland: Its History, Traditions and Folklore' David 'Dippie' Dixon referred to the marriage of Mary Amos of Shank House and Joseph Turnbull of Netherton. He recounted how, after the ceremony at Alnham Church, the 60 strong bridal party set out in the direction of the nearly 3 mile distant Shank House. On reaching the top of the hill, the bride's mother appeared waving a large, brightly coloured handkerchief, the prize for the first runner to reach the house. Off the young men went, jumping the tussocks and floundering through the bogs. Getting hot, they threw off their coats, hats and scarves and these were gathered up by the party stragglers. The race, known as 'The Running for the Kail', was won by Jack of Linshiels and, when everyone had reached the house, there was a great feast. The dancing went on deep into the night. Was this the 'foundation stone' of fell running in Northumberland? Now turn right and head towards the buildings, passing over a cattle grid and through a five bar gate, before turning left through the farmyard and over a step stile. Turn right, towards a shelter belt of trees on the northern side of the farm buildings, pass through and emerge almost immediately above the deep valley of the Shank Burn. Follow the track which descends the steep sided Green Knowe, crossing the burn by a small wooden footbridge and, once through the gate on the other side, start the stiff climb to the top of Little Dod. After pausing to admire the surrounding hills, continue across the barely noticeable 386 metre high top of Little Dod and, on reaching the arrowed fingerpost (**GR NT950142**), keep straight on, following in the footsteps of all those traders, drovers, smugglers and thieves who passed this way so many years ago.

5. Once you have reached the crest of the hill and just before the track starts its descent towards the upper reaches of the Breamish Valley, a green track (**GR NT946144**) leaves the Salter's Road, to your right, heading up the slopes of Shill Moor, initially towards a small rocky outcrop. Keep with this winding track and, when the fence and the five bar gate are reached, go through and turn left. Keep with the fence and continue across the grass and heather covered summit ridge to the 528 metre high top of Shill Moor. Capped with a rambling cairn and a trig point, this is a magnificent viewpoint. Here, high above a 90° turn in the course of the River Breamish, The Cheviot, Hedgehope Hill, Comb Fell and Cushat Law are the stars of a dazzling show, ably supported by Hogdon Law and Dunmoor Hill. To the east, the Northumberland North Sea coast makes a distant appearance. Time to drag yourself away, so cross back over to the eastern side of the fence and, with the cairn now to your back, head in an easterly direction towards the 'nose' of this splendid hill (**GR NT946154**). The views eastwards towards Brough Law and the Breamish Valley are well worth soaking up. Soon you will join a green track, heading to your right, which takes a twisting course down the lush, green slopes of the 'nose'. In time, you will see a small walkers cairn, looking suspiciously like a 'spot on the tip of the nose', and this is your next objective. Keep with the track and this eventually culminates at a tarmac road and the aptly named Snout End! Turn right along the 'private' road, passing, on the left, a fine plantation of Scots pine. Once past Alnhammoor, you are again crossing the bailey bridge and are well on your way to the buildings of Hartside Farm. One final short, sharp climb and you will be back to base with a 'rosy glow' of contentment.

Rowan tree and Alnhammoor.

FGS Grading

Grading is F9 [D1, N2, T2, R2, H2]

Distance	1	6 – 12 miles
Navigation	2	Competent navigation skills needed
Terrain	2	25 -50% on graded track or path 50 – 75% off / single track
Remoteness	2	Countryside not in close proximity to habitation – less than 20% of the route within 2 miles
Height	2	Over 125 ft per mile

WALK 5: THE WINDING ROAD TO WINDY GYLE

The summit of Windy Gyle lies 3 miles away from the nearest public road and is barely a hop, skip and a jump from the border between England and Scotland. It is the fourth highest of the Cheviot Hills and the only one over the magical 2000 feet mark to which Scotland can lay half a claim. This walk takes an unusual and less than direct route to the cairn crowned summit of this elemental hill, revealing along the way a variety of the many elements that make the hills of Upper Coquetdale so extra special.

DISTANCE: 10.25 miles (16.5 km)
ASCENT: 1837 feet (560 metres)
TERRAIN: A mixture of paths and tracks, some green, some gravel, one partially paved and a couple potentially muddy along with one stretch of tarmac
TIME: 4.5 hours
START: Near Windyhaugh, Upper Coquetdale (GR NT865109)

Grid References

Roadside	865 109
Barrow Burn	871 111
Clennell Street	875 137
Salter's Road	886 154
Clennell Street	875 157
Bridleway	859 148
Roadside	865 109

FGS Grading

Grading is F9 [D1, N2, T2, R2, H2]

THE WALK

1. Park on the small area of grass on the left hand side of the valley road, a few hundred metres beyond the telephone box which is located near to the farmstead of Barrowburn. On the opposite bank of the River Coquet, hidden behind a strand of trees, lies Windyhaugh farm, once a mill for the monks of Newminister. Sandwiches packed and boot laces tied and it is time to head a short distance back down the narrow road, as far as the five bar gate on your left, signposted ` Public Bridleway Middle Hill 1½ Border Ridge 4`. Pass through the gate and follow the track towards Barrowburn, keeping to the left of the buildings. Prior to 1935, the road through the valley passed this way, before turning through the farmyard on its way down stream towards Alwinton. Leave the route of the old road behind and pass through the shallow ford, or, if you prefer to keep your boots dry, cross the small wooden footbridge, continuing uphill past the wooden and stone buildings on your left. The stone building, now used as a camping barn, housed Windyhaugh School, relocated from its original accommodation in a converted byre at Windyhaugh farm. The school, which remained here until 1971, provided education for the children of Upper Coquetdale, from farms such as Uswayford, Trows, Rowhope, Carshope, Carlcroft and Fairhaugh. The wooden building, now named The Deer Hut, was the two bedroomed schoolhouse. Next to these buildings stand the bare remains of a farm or shepherd's house dating back to at least 1640 and last occupied in 1914. Once past the buildings and assuming that the five bar gate is closed, breath in and coax your hips through the extremely tight `squeeze stile`, keeping with the track as it first climbs uphill before dropping down to the Barrow Burn **(GR NT871111)**. The track meanders alongside the burn for a short distance and then begins its sharp climb towards the distant forest edge.

2. Once at the top of the rise, turn around and enjoy the superb view back towards Barrowburn and the River Coquet. Downhill, to your left, lies the narrow valley of the Usway Burn, dominated by the bulk of Shillhope Law. Turn back to face the forest and cross over the ladder stile. Do not follow the main track which heads downhill to the isolated holiday let of Fairhaugh, taking instead the green track immediately to your left, in the direction of the top of Middle Hill. After a short distance, just before the 396 metre summit is reached, your route veers to the right and tumbles downhill to join a muddy track arriving from Fairhaugh, away to your right. This junction is marked with a directional fingerpost. Turn left, and soon you will emerge out of the forest. Ignore the fingerpost a little way ahead choosing instead to follow the quad track up and over the top of the small hill lying immediately ahead of you, shown on the Ordnance Survey map as `The Middle`. From the top there are superb views of the way ahead. Now continue straight on until you reach the junction with the ancient drover's road of Clennell Street **(GR NT875137)** and the gravel road leading to Uswayford farm. It is hard to believe that, over 400 years ago, this quiet place, known in medieval times as Oswold Myddle (i.e. Usway Middle), was one of the most important track junctions of the border hills and that a drover's inn stood here in this empty landscape. Now turn right along the track towards the farm, some ¾ mile from here, skirting the steep south eastern slopes of Hazely Law. Ignore the side track which climbs towards the forest and soon the farm buildings will come into view, nestling below the western flanks of Bloodybush Edge. When William Weaver Tomlinson wrote his "Comprehensive Guide to Northumberland " in 1888, Uswayford was just a shepherd's hut. It is one of the most remote farms in the Northumberland, has in the past served as a rainfall station for the Metrological Office and now provides welcome `bed and breakfast` accommodation. You would be hard pressed to find a more secluded and peaceful situation.

3. Where the track turns to the right and drops downhill to ford the Usway Burn, leave the track by heading left along a thin path towards the wooden footbridge straddling the burn. Once over, immediately cross the step stile on your left and head uphill, turning away from the fence, to pick up a thin path, in essence little more than a sheep trace, which heads in a northerly direction high above the Usway Burn. Soon you will reach the point where the Clay Burn joins the Usway Burn. It is a most delightful place and one where you may want to pause awhile. Cross over the Clay Burn, at its narrowest point, and follow the path which climbs uphill, turning slightly to the right as it heads towards the forest. At the top of the short hill cross over the step stile, with the adjacent `yellow arrow` indicating the way ahead. Continue along the forest ride, on a clear path, and before long you will reach a sign post indicating that you have now joined the Salter's Road **(GR NT886154)**, an ancient track which crosses the Cheviot Hills from the tiny Northumberland village of Alnham to Cocklawfoot in Scotland. Your route heads west so, turning to your left, follow the track, initially through trees and then over open hillside high above the Usway Burn. On finally reaching the Usway Burn, cross over to the western bank, via a wooden footbridge, and, facing the fine circular sheep stell, turn left. There are few really big waterfalls in the Cheviot Hills, but in this remote valley, now hidden deep in the forest, Davidson's Linn is an impressive sight as it falls away below your feet. This is a place to linger a while as you listen to the sound of water tumbling into peat brown pools. Not far from here, on Inner Hare Cleugh, a few grey boulders mark the site of the area's best known illicit kiln for drying malted barley, `Rory's Still `.

4. The path leaves the burn parallel with the waterfall, climbing uphill to your right and re-enters the forest on a muddy, uphill track. You will need to duck, dive and weave your way through the trees in order to avoid the worst of the mud but before long you will reach a gravel forest road and a directional fingerpost. Turn left along this road for a very short distance and then head back into the trees via another muddy track on your right. Eventually, after much slipping and sliding on an uphill trajectory, you will emerge once again into full daylight, as you first cross over two step stiles in quick succession, and then, within a few strides, your route merges with Clennell Street **(GR NT875157).** The hills lining the border between England and Scotland are now in sight and, after little more than a quarter of a mile of gentle uphill walking, the post and wire `international` boundary fence is reached. This is Hexpethgate, more commonly called the Border Gate, one of seventeen border crossings in the Cheviot Hills mentioned in a state paper of 1543. It stands at 542 metres above sea level and was one of the meeting places for the Wardens of the Middle Marches. Keeping on English soil, turn left and begin your easy climb of just over one mile, along the route of the Pennine Way, to the summit of Windy Gyle. Most of the way is paved with stone slaps reclaimed from derelict cotton mills. The 619 metre summit lies in Scotland, so a cross border excursion must be made on reaching the small gate and step stile.

5. History positively seeps from the triangulation pillar topped Windy Gyle and the surrounding area, where for centuries armies fought bloody battles, families stole cattle from one another and violence was a way of life. In 1585, at a meeting of the Wardens of the Middle Marches, Lord Francis Russell was murdered near to this spot and the large Bronze Age burial cairn on the top of the hill was named Russell's Cairn to commemorate the deadly event. The views from this hill of dual nationality are spectacular. In his lovely little 1950 booklet `A Guide to the Cheviot Hills`, F. R. Banks enthused "…..from Cheviot in the north west, by Comb Fell, Hedgehope and Dunmoor Hill, Shill Moor (east) and the flattish hump of Bloodybush Edge, Wether Cairn and the distant Simonside Hills, Shillhope Law (south) and yet more distant Pennines, and Thirlmoor (south west), to the Carter Fell range". Weather permitting, you should be able to spot a few more besides. You will not want to leave, but leave you must. Return to the fence, step stile and gate and continue, initially straight ahead, down a clear green and rutted track. Soon, a public bridleway, named on the Ordnance Survey map as `Split the Deil`, will arrive from your right. This name first appeared on the 1899 second edition of the Ordnance Survey map of the area, the track having been given no name at all on the 1866 first edition. Many earlier maps had referred to this track by the name of `Maiden Cross`, and this was, like Hexpethgate, listed in the 1543 state paper as one of the seventeen border crossings. It seems a great pity that this ancient name should have fallen into disuse and is now virtually forgotten.

6. As you continue your descent, the public bridleway **(GR NT859148)** heads towards Scotchman's Ford, whilst your route turns right when the second of two directional fingerposts is reached, heading in a generally southerly direction down the broad green ridge between the Trows and Wardlaw Burns. This is wonderfully relaxing walking over closely cropped grass heading in the direction of the valley of the Rowhope Burn surrounded by fine views. Eventually you will join a clear rutted track and, in time, the second of two five bar gates will deliver you to the valley and the fording of the Trows Burn. If you still wish to keep your boots dry, you can cross either of the adjoining footbridges. Continuing in the same direction you will immediately pass, on your right, the 1960`s built Trows farmhouse, replacing the original farmhouse which stood on the left hand side of the track. This building is now used for storage purposes. Like many farms in the Upper Coquetdale area, these buildings are now owned by the MoD. The track turns to tarmac and soon you will pass the exceptionally neat and still very active farmstead of Rowhope. It is now less than one mile of delightful walking alongside the chattering Rowhope Burn before the single track road through Coquetdale is reached. Where the roads merge, known as Slymefoot or White Bridge, take the left hand option and, after passing some sheep pens and the starting line of the annual Windy Gyle Fell Race, you will be back beside the tree enclosed buildings of Windyhaugh. Now for the next walk!

The Clay Burn where it joins the Usway Burn.

The footbridge at Uswayford.

FGS Grading

Grading is F9 [D1, N2, T2, R2, H2]

Distance	1	6 – 12 miles
Navigation	2	Competent navigation skills needed
Terrain	2	25 -50% on graded track or path 50 – 75% off / single track
Remoteness	2	Countryside not in close proximity to habitation – less than 20% of the route within 2 miles
Height	2	Over 125 ft per mile

WALK 6: THE HIGH CIRCUIT OF THE USWAY BURN

The buildings of Shillmoor nestle beside the River Coquet where the impressive Shillhope Law dominates the narrow, twisting valley of the Usway Burn. Further to the north, Yarnspath Law rises above the remote farmstead of Uswayford. This walk links together these two fine hills and offers a bucket full of outstanding views from the high horseshoe shaped circuit of this, the most delightful of Cheviot burns.

DISTANCE:10.25 miles (16.5 km)
ASCENT: 2280 feet (695 metres)
TERRAIN: Mixed fell (sometimes boggy), some good, green tracks and the occasional gravel track
TIME: 5 hours
START: Near Shillmoor, Upper Coquetdale (GR NT885077)

Grid References

Near Shillmoor	885 077
Track junction	890 095
Clennell Street	897 106
Track junction	893 117
Track/path junction	888 131
Gate	892 138
Stile	879 128
Track junction	882 125
Gate	873 101
Near Shillmoor	885 077

FGS Grading

Grading is F9 [D1, N2, T2, R2, H2]

THE WALK

1. Park beside the River Coquet, immediately before the road bridge. On with the boots and head over the bridge, turning right along the road past two stone faced houses on your left and then the buildings of Shillmoor. This farmstead is now owned by the MoD so do not be surprised to see an Army vehicle or two as you pass through the five bar gate and over the concrete bridge across the Usway Burn. Follow the gravel track, ignoring the dry stone wall hugging public foot-path which heads straight on towards Alwinton, and soon you will begin to feel the sharper gradient tugging on your legs. You have now begun the 2 mile long and unrelenting climb of the oddly named Copper Snout, once a spur of the area's best known drove road, Clennell Street. Already the views are opening up, with the steep sided Shillhope Law, away to your left, being of particular scenic inter-est. At around the 420 metre contour (**GR NT890095**) be careful to follow the track as it turns to the left and not the track which heads straight on. A directional fingerpost points your way. With the summit of Saughy Hill now in view, the track begins to cross flatter ground where the trees of the Kidland Forest can be seen ahead. Once over the step stile, the second since starting your climb, turn right and a rather `damp` path will eventually bring you to the gravel track of Clennell Street (**GR NT897106**). This is the king of the Cheviot drove roads, used by the Cistercian monks of Newminster to reach their upland sheep pastures on Kidland and named in a monastic charter of 1181 as `the great road of Yarn-speth`.

2. Turn left and begin your first taste of the day of `the great road of Yarnspeth`, a `road` you will follow northwards for just short of 1 mile. To your right lies the 5,190 acre Kidland Forest, originally planted between 1953 and 1987, and now in the process of being harvested and replanted. A total of 2,965 acres of the forest are owned by the Forestry Commission, with the remaining areas being in private ownership. When the track splits in two (**GR NT893117**), just prior to Hosden Hope and splendid views to Shillhope Law, take the right hand spur which heads through a stretch of harvested and freshly replanted forest. Keep with the main track, ignoring, after approximately 200 metres, the side track to your right which drops away to the hidden cottage of Whiteburnshank, now used as an Outdoor Centre. After nearly 1 mile of walking, when the track begins to bend away to the right, follow the thin path which cuts through the small gap in the trees to your left (**GR NT888131**). Cross over the step stile and as your feet touch the very wet ground on the other side, turn right. This area is the watershed of the West Burn which, on meeting with the East Burn, becomes the White Burn eventually drain-ing into the River Alwin. With the heather clad hillside to your left and the forest edge to your right continue across the damp ground towards the saddle between your first summit of the day, Yarnspath Law, and Bloodybush Edge. On reaching the post and wire fence and the five bar gate (**GR NT892138**), turn left and then, almost immediately, cross over the step stile. From here there are good views to the whaleback of The Cheviot and the green expanse of the Uswayford Forest.

3. You are now climbing generally south westwards over normally boggy terrain towards the 543 metre high top of Yarnspath Law. Continue over the barely noticeable top until you reach the point where the hillside begins to fall sharply downhill. Take time to pause and to soak up the superb views across an ocean of green, rounded hills, towards the border between England and Scotland. On a clear, bright day these are the Cheviot Hills at their very best. Follow the fence and the faint quad track downhill, over mat grass covered slopes, until you reach a clear track and a step stile into the forest (**GR NT879128**). You are now back on Clennell Street as you re-enter the forest and follow this ancient and, at this point, rutted 'road' south eastwards for approximately half a mile, until you reach another track, on your right (**GR NT882125**). Follow this track, over level ground at first and then steeply downhill through a couple of hairpin bends, to the former shepherds cottage of Fairhaugh,. Turn right behind the shuttered cottage, which is now used as a holiday let, and cross the delightful Usway Burn, via the wooden footbridge. You will be happy to pause on the bridge and watch the burn dance across a series of small waterfalls before it then drops down into the peat brown pool, immediately beneath the bridge. Now turn left and follow the track as it soon climbs away from the burn and into the forest. At the top of the incline, cross over the ladder stile and step out of the forest. From here there are great views towards Shillhope Law and a distant River Coquet.

4. Your route now heads south eastwards, rising steeply up a clear green quad track towards the 433 metre high Kyloe Shin. The absolute top lies slightly to the left of the track, just before your route begins to head back downhill. Pick the easiest way down the south western slope of the hill and, when more even ground is reached, follow the thin path and then the faint quad track which head across the saddle towards Shillhope Law. Eventually, the pleasant grassy track starts to slowly rise uphill, coming to an abrupt halt at a five bar gate (**GR NT873101**). Time to give the legs some serious exercise! Climb over the gate and follow the path which rises sharply alongside a post and wire fence. As the grass covered slope becomes heather clad hillside, the underfoot conditions deteriorate until eventually a thin path turns away to the right to emerge at the trig point on the 501 metre high summit of Shillhope Law. The trig point sits on top of the remains of a large Bronze Age cairn which is made of loose angular stones and measures approximately 16-20 metres in diameter. This is a Scheduled Ancient Monument. A modern stone wall provides useful shelter against the elements. Be sure to venture away from the trig point for some spectacular views of Upper Coquetdale and the Border Ridge. To the north east, a very distant Cheviot is visible.

5. With your back to the trig point and facing south, take the thin path, which angles away to the left, and enjoy the short and easy downhill stretch to the col between Shillhope Law and Inner Hill. Climb over the post and wire fence, via the gate, and head the short distance to the top of Inner Hill. The hillsides fall steeply away to your left from where there are superb, near vertical views down to the wandering valley of the Usway Burn. Continue over the top and then begin your descent back down to the valley. The fence on your right in turn becomes a stone wall and all too soon you reach the gravel track running alongside the Usway Burn. Turn right and follow the track behind the farmstead of Shillmoor and, when the tarmac road is reached, continue to your right past the two stone faced houses. You are back alongside the River Coquet and within a matter of minutes your walk high above the Usway Burn is already just a happy memory.

Shillhope Law from below Saughy Hill.

Hosden Burn

FGS Grading

Grading is F9 [D1, N2, T2, R2, H2]

Distance	1	6 – 12 miles
Navigation	2	Competent navigation skills needed
Terrain	2	25 -50% on graded track or path 50 – 75% off / single track
Remoteness	2	Countryside not in close proximity to habitation – less than 20% of the route within 2 miles
Height	2	Over 125 ft per mile

WALK 7: THE HETHPOOL BORDER CIRCUIT

The Pennine Way clings to the border fence as it wanders over the high hills rising to the west of the beautiful and remote College Valley. The tiny settlement of Hethpool sits at the northern end of the valley, in the shadow of the towering Newton Tors. Between the valley and the `international` border with Scotland lies a series of wonderfully rounded hills, many of which are sprinkled with the relics of a distant and turbulent past. This walk explores some of the history of these hills whilst tasting the delights of two long distance footpaths. It even dares to set foot on `foreign` soil.

DISTANCE: 9 miles (14.5 km)
ASCENT: 2166 feet (660 metres)
TERRAIN: Mainly good green tracks/paths with some stretches of tarmac
TIME: 4.5 hours
START: Hethpool, College Valley (GR NT893280)

Grid References

Hethpool	893 280
Road	877 269
Wideopen Head	861 265
White Swire	853 268
Tuppie's Sike	859 276
Signpost	883 282
Hethpool	893 280

FGS Grading

Grading is F9 [D1, N2, T2, R2, H2]

THE WALK

1. There is a special parking area just beyond the row of cottages at Hethpool, immediately after the cattle grid at the end of the public road. Whilst the hamlet has a history dating back to 1242, its present character is largely determined by a group of buildings belonging to the Arts & Crafts style of the early 20th century. The splendid Hethpool House was built in 1919, with the distinctive conical roofed tower being added in 1928. A ruined tower still stands in the garden of the house and this was described in the 1957 edition of 'The Buildings of England: Northumberland' by Nikolaus Pevsner as "a ruin of a late 14th century tower more remarkable for its picturesque than its archaeological value". He added that it was "set at the end of a well tended garden, against a glorious background of hills". So, surrounded by those glorious hills, start your day by heading south, along the narrow road, towards the head of the valley. After little more than 200 metres, on the extensive area of grass to your right, you will see a number of stones lying in a fallen position. These are the remains of a Neolithic stone circle. Once at the end of the small plantation, on your right and just under half a mile after starting, you must leave the easy valley walking behind and, following the 'permissive path' signposted 'Great Hetha ¾', commence your first climb of the day. It will certainly not be the last.

2. The path follows the edge of the plantation and, on reaching the stone wall at the top edge of the trees, turns to the left to make the final 'assault' on the summit of Great Hetha, via a thin, disintegrating path and then a good track. The 343 metre high summit, marked by a walkers cairn, stands at the north eastern end of the hill from where there are fine views of the College Valley and the surrounding hills. The remains of a strongly defended Iron Age hill fort lie on the top, surrounded by two ramparts of earth and stone. There is an entrance, on the north west side, with traces of an in-turned bank where it passes through the inner rampart. Continue across the broad green ridge, in a south westerly direction, following the route of the 'permissive path', which is not always clear underfoot. When the white gable end of Trowupburn farm comes into view, way below, descend the hill, heading to the left of the cluster of eight trees. Cross over the nearby step stile and on reaching the road (**GR NT877269**) turn left. Follow the road downhill, passing behind the farm buildings, to join a public footpath which crosses the Trowup Burn from the east and climbs diagonally up the hillside to the west. This is your route. After 200 metres, leave the rough track behind and head uphill on a subsidiary track through an extensive area of gorse. This is at its magnificent best in springtime. When the gradient eases, with an oblong stone sheep enclosure to your right, be sure to follow the green track which angles slightly to your left, keeping to the right of the small rise.

3. You are now cutting across the flanks of Madam Law where, on the night of 24/25th March 1943, a Dornier Do 217E-4 aircraft crashed following a raid on the docks at Leith, Edinburgh. On the same night, a Junkers Ju 88 aircraft crashed close to Rig Cairn, high above the Linhope Burn, and a Spitfire crashed into Bellyside Hill on the north side of The Cheviot. In total nine young airmen died in the Cheviot Hills that night. On reaching Wideopen Head **(GR NT861265),** which lies at the south eastern end of the saddle between White Law and Madam Law, the track you have been following heads straight through the gate, eventually stepping into Scotland via the ancient crossing of the White Swire. Before you continue your journey by turning left, why not make the minor detour to the 397 metre high summit of Madam Law. Pass through the gate, turn right and head the short distance uphill to the cairn crowned top. Enjoy the panorama and then return the same way. Once back at the other side of the gate, you must turn right to follow the track uphill, with the post and wire fence to your right, towards the 429 metre high summit of White Law. For centuries the exact position of the border between England and Scotland was the subject of considerable `debate`, and in his 1924 book `The Border Line`, James Logan Mack said, "As the watershed here controls the nationality of the soil, Scotland now claims the actual peak of White Law as its own". Not quite. The true summit stands a few metres to the north of the small gate through the border fence and, therefore, lies within English territory. Now go through the gate and plant your boots firmly on `foreign` soil. The views are outstanding. Looking south, the border fence climbs up the beautiful Steer Rig, caught between the Halterburn Valley to the west and the valley of the Trowup Burn to the east, heading towards Black Hag and the broad girth of The Curr. A plethora of small, curvaceous hills disappear into the Scottish distance.

4. You are standing on the route of the Pennine Way, waymarked over its entire length with an acorn symbol, and, with your back to the gate, turn to your right and head towards the ladder stile at Whitelaw Nick, some 300 metres away. Cross over the stile and immediately start your descent on a thin path alongside the dry stone wall `Border Line`. This is the watershed of the Witchcleugh Burn which trickles westwards to join the Halter Burn less than a mile away. Keep with the thin path and as you reach the top of the next incline, you will be re-joining the track you left a short while ago at Wideopen Head. This is the White Swire **(GR NT853268),** first documented in 1222, one of the seventeen border crossings listed in a state paper of 1543 and a point of passage favoured by generations of reivers and drovers. Continue with the Pennine Way, but be careful to make a short diversion, to the left, after some 100 metres of walking at the point where the excellent green track begins its downward journey. Here stand the Stob Stanes, known locally as the `Gypsy Stobs`, which mark the spot where the gypsy kings and queens were traditionally crowned. The larger of the two stones, which is still upright, measures 1.65 metres in height. The true purpose of the stones is unknown, although they may have marked a medieval border line between England and Scotland. They may have had a more mysterious ritualistic purpose. Return to the main track, by turning right, and head downhill for a short distance until the signposted St. Cuthbert's Way is reached.

5. Now turn right and start your 4 mile journey back to the College Valley. You will climb uphill on a good track towards the border and before long you will, once again, be stepping into England. A St. Cuthbert's Way signpost will welcome you `home`. Opened in 1996, St. Cuthbert's Way links together the religious sites of Melrose Abbey and Lindisfarne and is normally walked in a west to east direction. You will be going with the flow of `pilgrims` for virtually all of the return route. Within 20 metres, a thread thin path cuts away to the left heading towards your next vantage point, Eccles Cairn, from where there are superb views back into Scotland. If the air is clear, the triple tops of the Eildon Hills will be plain to see. Return to St. Cuthbert's Way by heading in a south easterly direction, towards the directional fingerpost, and, once reached, continue downhill, to your left, to cross the damp ground of Tuppie's Sike **(GR NT859276)**. The path rises away from the sike, heading towards the north west corner of the small plantation, climbing under the dark green canopy via a step stile. After all the wide open vistas enjoyed over the last 6 miles, the tight, dark confines of the plantation are mildly claustrophobic. Daylight will come as a relief!

6. A thin path cuts down Scaldhill Shank, in a north easterly direction, crossing Shank's Sike, passing through a five bar gate and rising as a track to another five bar gate. The track then heads towards the buildings of Elsdonburn, contouring the lower flanks of Ell's Knowe. As you approach the bungalow go through yet another five bar gate, first swinging left with the track and then turning right past a signpost. Ignore the route to `Elsdonburn Shank`. You are now alongside the Elsdon Burn on a good tarmac road and you will stay with this for just over half a mile of pleasant walking. Eventually, the road merges with the Trowupburn access road and, just beyond this junction, a signpost **(GR NT883282)** points the way, via a `permissive path`, to Great Hetha. This is your route, although your destination is the somewhat nearer Little Hetha. Leave the road to your right and begin your climb up the green hillside, alongside a post and wire fence. When you reach a directional fingerpost, turn left and almost before you have time to say "Iron Age defended settlement" you have reached the 210 metre high summit. The remains of this settlement stand on a spur surrounded by steep slopes and two ramparts. This is an impressive site with excellent all

50

round views. Return to the tarmac road by the same route. Now turn right and continue your Elsdon Burn hugging journey in the company of beautiful rolling hills. When you reach, after ¾ mile, the single track road to Westnewton, turn right. As you make your way onwards watch out for the small post box, set into the reverse side of a circular stone pillar to your left, and, as you re-enter the College Valley nearing the end of your day in the hills, admire the picture postcard cottages standing to your right. These 1926 built cottages have been described as "among the finest cottages to be seen anywhere in Northumberland". What do you think?

Part of the Neolithic stone circle in the College Valley.

FGS Grading

Grading is F9 [D1, N2, T2, R2, H2]

Distance	1	6 – 12 miles
Navigation	2	Competent navigation skills needed
Terrain	2	25 -50% on graded track or path 50 – 75% off / single track
Remoteness	2	Countryside not in close proximity to habitation – less than 20% of the route within 2 miles
Height	2	Over 125 ft per mile

WALK 8: HIGH ALONG THE BORDER LINE

The ancient drove road, once known as `the Clattering Path`, climbs steeply away from the River Coquet and follows a high level route to the border between England and Scotland. The more recently created long distance footpath, the Pennine Way, follows the border through the high Cheviot Hills on a journey of splendid isolation. This walk links together `the Clattering Path` and the Pennine Way, crossing the summits of Swineside Law, Mozie Law, Beefstand Hill, Lamb Hill and Carlcroft Hill. The views along the way are outstanding.

DISTANCE: 10 miles (16.1 km)
ASCENT: 1739 feet (530 metres)
TERRAIN: Good green tracks, paved millstone slabs with intermittent worn peat paths, thin paths through areas of grassland.
TIME: 5 hours
START: Slymefoot (White Bridge), Upper Coquetdale (GR NT859114)

Grid References

Bridge	859 114
Stile	839 131
Signpost	835 149
Refuge Hut	804 129
Track Junction	809 129
Carlcroft Burn	838 117
Signpost	849 116
Bridge	859 114

FGS Grading

Grading is F9 [D1, N2, T2, R2, H2]

THE WALK

1. Park beside the bridge straddling the Rowhope Burn, next to the private road leading to the remote farm of Uswayford. In the 18th century, close to this spot, the infamous Slymefoot public house rattled to the sound of local sheep farmers spending the long winter days gambling and drinking illicit whisky. Bootlaces tied, cross the bridge and then the step stile next to the five bar gate, following the uphill track signposted " The Street. Border Ridge 3". This is the ancient high level drove road, shown on General Roy's 1775 map as `the Clattering Path` but now known as `the Street`, which runs from Upper Coquetdale to Hownam in the Kale Water Valley. As you rise, alongside the post and wire fence, the views are already beginning to open up. At the top of the hill, cross the stile to your left and keep with the fence as it heads west for a short distance before turning downhill in a north westerly direction. After crossing the damp ground of the infant Dreary Sike, your route again climbs uphill, with the guiding fence firmly on your right. As you gain height and cut cross the slopes of Hindside Knowe and Bought Law, always staying close up and personal with the fence, the views towards Windy Gyle and down into the deep valley of the Rowhope Burn are a delight. The views towards the border continue to draw you on as you head over easy ground towards Swineside Law, your first `top` of the day. `The Street` does not cross the actual summit of this 457 metre high hill so, on reaching the 440 metre contour **(GR NT839131)** where a small stile crosses the fence to your right, be sure to make the very short detour, to your left, to claim your first top of the day. A faint track leads you there and back.

2. On returning to `the Street`, turn left and your route heads downhill to a small col where you cross to the opposite side of the fence. Now begins the climb up Black Braes, so take a deep breath and a sip of high energy drink! On finally reaching the gate and the step stile, take a few minutes to admire the wonderful view `from whence you came`. To the south east, some four crow flown miles away, the `full bodied` Shillhope Law dominates the distant skyline. Continue along the rutted track, which soon reaches level ground and the steep slopes, on your left, falling away to the Easthope Burn. This burn carries rainwater from your next hill, Mozie Law, down into the Carlcroft Burn and then into the River Coquet. Once over the next step stile and, after a further 400 metres, on reaching the `Pennine Way` signpost at Plea Knowe **(GR NT835149)**, it is time to turn left across yet another step stile. The signpost indicates that your next hill of the day, Mozie Law, is a mere ½ mile away. Near to this spot there is a large cross dyke, consisting of a 130 metre long bank and ditch, dating from the medieval or post-medieval period. The exact purpose of this dyke is not known. The post and wire fence, now on your right, marks the border between England and Scotland and you will stay with this until you reach the mountain refuge hut on Yearning Saddle, some 2¾ miles from here.

3. Writing in his 1985 book `Wainwright on the Pennine Way`, the author, known affectionately as `AW`, said that "an absence of landmarks makes this section a monotonous treadmill" adding that "there are some wet places but the ground is generally dry and vegetated by grass and heather with an occasional sighting of the lovely cloudberry". Since then, intermittent sections of stone pathway have been constructed to prevent erosion on this, Britain's most popular long distance footpath. You will make up your own mind as to whether or not the journey is as monotonous as AW would have you believe! You may be more inclined to agree with a certain Tom Stephenson who , when he first proposed the Pennine Way in 1935, rated the Cheviot Hills as his favourite walking area in the country. If you are lucky, you may just catch a glimpse of the feral goats which roam this area of the Cheviot Hills. As you wander over the high ground, you will feel totally alone except, perhaps, for the occasional Pennine Way walker hauling his or her weary feet over the final few miles of an epic journey. When Christopher John Wright wrote his `Guide to the Pennine Way` in 1967, two years after the route was officially opened, the border fence was non-existent in many places. So, in order to aid navigation along the way, numerous cairns were built with peat sods and these were topped with temporary notice boards. The undistinguished 552 and 562 metre tops of Mozie Law and Beefstand Hill will pass by almost unnoticed as you enjoy the easy going. Pause for a moment on the top of Beefstand Hill and enjoy the panorama, to the north east, towards the Cheviot heartland, where The Cheviot, Hedgehope Hill and the Schil stretch out across the horizon.

4. After reaching the trig point topped 511 metre high summit of Lamb Hill, just a few metres across the border in Scotland, a gentle downhill stretch will bring you to the mountain refuge hut **(GR NT804129)** on Yearning Saddle. This is the perfect spot for a break and to take time out to savour the final remnants of your time on the border ridge. There are some superb views across the flimsy border into Scotland. Leave the `comfort` of the hut by following the fingerpost way-marked green track in an easterly direction until the track spits in two **(GR NT809129)**. Take the left hand `public footpath` spur as it makes its thin winding way, over skylark scattered grasslands, towards a circular sheep stell in the narrow valley of the Blind Burn. A series of well spaced marker posts guide the way, so be sure to always keep a look out for the next one in line. Further down the Blind Burn Valley, squeezed between the lower slopes of Yearning Law and Carlcroft Hill, lie the foundations of a single building, measuring 20 metres by 3.5 metres. This, together with the adjoining circular enclosure, formed part of a medieval or post-medieval settlement. Cross the burn and follow the way marked path as it rises steeply towards the upper slopes of Carlcroft Hill. As you climb, glance across to the south west where the bare remains of the grandly named Yearning Hall stand with only a cluster of non-deciduous trees for company. Despite bearing a mildly pretentious name, this was nothing more than a remote, two roomed dwelling, with a large byre and a pigsty. It was last occupied at the beginning of the 1940`s, when it was purchased by the MoD.

5. Eventually, on reaching a fence and a step stile, turn left and make the short diversion to the unmarked 447 metre high top of Carlcroft Hill. There are good views to Windy Gyle. Return to and cross over the step stile and continue straight ahead over closely cropped grass covered slopes. There is no discernible path, so continue to contour the hillside whilst heading slightly down the slope towards yet another step stile. Once across, head towards the bottom right hand corner of the field. Cross the stile, next to a five bar gate, and continue you journey downhill on a clear track towards the farm of Carlcroft. The waymarked path passes through a series of gates, keeping to the immediate left of the farm buildings, and then crosses the Carlcroft Burn **(GR NT838117)** via a wooden footbridge. You must now take the left hand track, climbing in an easterly direction along a public bridleway, just to the north of the River Coquet and the narrow, twisting valley road. After 400 metres, pass through a wooden gate and continue in the same general direction.

6. When you catch sight of the fledgling plantation covering the lower part of Stogie's Cleugh, be sure to head uphill, aiming to the left of the circular sheep stell. Above the top end of the plantation you will find a small wooden gate and an adjoining step stile. Cross over and follow the public bridleway sign, climbing to your right towards the next directional fingerpost, where you must then turn sharp left. A further 50 metres on and on reaching another directional marker, turn right along a splendid green track **(GR NT849116)**. This track soon merges with `the Street` just before you reach the step stile, which you crossed on your outward journey, and the exhilarating last downhill stretch to the bridge at Slymefoot. This is the final section of the annual 9 mile Windy Gyle Fell Race, and just over half a mile of superb, eye rattling descent to the finish line near to the sheep pens on the road to the farmsteads of Windyhaugh and Barrowburn. Enjoy every step of the track back to the valley floor and your starting point. You might just be tempted to run all the way!

The Rowhope Burn and the start of the walk.

FGS Grading

Grading is F9 [D1, N2, T2, R2, H2]

Distance	1	6 – 12 miles
Navigation	2	Competent navigation skills needed
Terrain	2	25 -50% on graded track or path 50 – 75% off / single track
Remoteness	2	Countryside not in close proximity to habitation – less than 20% of the route within 2 miles
Height	2	Over 125 ft per mile

APPENDIX

Ferguson Grading System (`FGS`)

1. Introduction
The FGS has been adopted as a means of assessing the nature and severity of the various walks in this book and the abilities and equipment needed to tackle each one safely. The FGS was developed by Stuart Ferguson, a long time fell and trail runner, climber, mountaineer, mountain-biker and general outdoor enthusiast. In the opinion of Trailguides the FGS is the most accurate and comprehensive grading system for comparing off-road walking, running and mountain-biking routes anywhere in the country.

2. The System
Tables 1 & 2, set out below, are used in order to give a grading to each route. Table 1 sets out three categories of country that a route could potentially cross, together with a range of factors that would need to be considered when tackling that route. The three categories are, Trail, Fell and Mountain, and after assessing which category best fits the route, a letter, either `T`, `F` or `M`, is allocated to that route. Where a route does not fit perfectly into one of the three categories the closest category is allocated.

Table 2 deals with five specific aspects of the route, distance, navigation, terrain, remoteness and height gain, and each one is allocated a letter, `D`, `N`, `T`, `R`, and `H`. Each letter is also given a severity score from the range 0-3 or 0-4, in respect of distance (`D`). The higher the number, the more severe the route. The five severity scores are then added together to give an overall score. The overall score is then put with the Table 1 category letter (i.e. `T`, `F` or `M`).

In order to show how the grading has been determined for each walk in this book, the five individual severity scores are set out, in square brackets, immediately after the actual grading. So, for example, Walk 6 The High Circuit of the Usway Burn has a grading of F9 [D1, N2, T2, R2, H2], indicating that it is a Fell Category walk with a total severity score of 9. This is made up of the five specific severity scores, for distance (`D`), navigation (`N`), terrain (`T`), remoteness (`R`) and height gain (`H`), of 1, 2, 2, 2 and 2 respectively. The highest total severity score which can be achieved is 16 and the lowest total severity score achievable is 0.

The table which accompanies the grading at the end of each walk sets out the specific factors, extracted from Table 2, that need to be considered when tackling that particular walk.

TABLE 1

	TRAIL	FELL	MOUNTAIN
Description	Lowland and forest areas including urban, cultivated and forested locations.	Moorlands and upland areas which may include some upland cultivated and forestry areas plus possibly remote locations.	Upland and mountain areas including remote and isolated locations.
Height	Not usually above 1,000 feet but may go up to 2,500 feet	Usually above 1,000 feet, up to 2,500 feet and above.	Usually above 2,500 feet and up to 4,000 feet.
Way-marking	Usually	Limited	None
Terrain	Usually graded paths, tracks and trails but may include some off-trail	May include some graded paths, tracks and trails but mainly off-trail	Virtually all off-trail
Height gain	Limited height gain	May include considerable height gain	May include some severe height gain.
Effects of weather	Very limited effect	May be prone to sudden weather changes	Extreme weather a possibility
Navigational skills	None to basic	Basic to competent	Competent to expert
Equipment	Walking shoes/boots. Possibly waterproofs Food and drink dependant upon route.	3/4 season walking boots. Full waterproof cover. Possibly map and compass dependant upon route. Food and drink dependant upon route.	Mountain boots. Full waterproof cover. Map and compass. Food and drink
Escape Routes	Yes	Some	Some to nil

TABLE 2

Score	0	1	2	3	4
Distance	Up to 6 miles	6 – 12 miles	12 – 18 miles	18 miles +	24 miles +
Navigation	No navigation skills needed	Basic navigation skills needed	Competent navigation skills needed	Expert navigation skills needed	
Terrain	75% + on graded track or path	50 – 75% on graded track or path 25 – 50% off track	25 -50% on graded track or path 50 – 75% off track	Under 25% on graded track or path Over 75% off track	
Remoteness	Urban	Countryside in fairly close proximity to habitation – at least 80% of the route within 2 miles	Countryside not in close proximity to habitation – less than 20% of the route within 2 miles	Remote, isolated location	
Height gain	Less than 100 ft per mile	Over 100 ft per mile	Over 125 ft per mile	Over 250 ft per mile	

Notes to Table 2

Graded paths = Well established paths with a stable surface.

. Escape routes = The opportunity to cut the route short and return to the start without completing the full course in the event of weather changes or unforeseen incidents.

The Author

Geoff Holland

Geoff is a Northumbrian by birth and for the last thirty three years has lived as a resident of Monkseaton, just a stone's throw from the North Sea coast. For most of his years he has enjoyed the outdoors as a hill walker, fell runner and mountain-biker. In particular he has developed a love for the hills of his home county, the Cheviots.

Over the years Geoff has written more than forty five walks and related outdoor articles which have appeared in such publications as "Country Walking" and "The Northumbrian" magazines along with a selection of his photographs. In addition seven of his 'North Tyneside Heritage Walks' have been published in leaflet form and as a further extension of his literary talents a number of his poems have appeared in magazines, journals and online.

Geoff's passion for the Cheviots has lead him to set-up and operate an acclaimed website dedicated to walking in the Cheviot Hills which is recognised as being as being one of the best walking sites in the North of England.

Geoff is married with two grown up children and one grandchild.

The author (light vest) competing in the Alwinton Shepherds Show Fell Race 1986

Trailguides Limited

So what's Trailguides all about then? Well, Trailguides is a small company that produces and publishes guide books and route guides for activity sports such as walking, mountain biking and trail running. The team here are all active participants in one or more of these activities and as such know what they like to see in a guide book or route guide. Hopefully it's the same as you .... otherwise we might go out of business.

Our aim is to produce guides that are as user-friendly, easy to use and provide as much information as possible and all in an entertaining manner. The aim is to increase the enjoyment of your chosen activity.

Being a small company, Trailguides have the flexibility and smallness to come up with new routes and ideas without having to worry about lengths of production runs to cover costs. With being virtually a "cottage industry", our size or more accurately, lack of it, allows us to produce guides that sell in their tens or in their hundreds. This gives us the freedom to open up routes that challenge and intrigue. Routes that appeal and fascinate us and will have the same effect on you.

So keep in touch, there will always be something new on the horizon.

If you've enjoyed following the routes in this guide and want news and details of other routes that are being developed by Trailguides then look at the company website at
www.trailguides.co.uk

Comments and, yes, criticisms, are always welcomed especially if you discover a change to a route. Contact us by email through the website or by post at Trailguides Limited, 35 Carmel Road South, Darlington, Co Durham DL3 8DQ.

Acknowledgements.

Are due to the online Northumbrian literary magazine
www.acknowledgedland.com in which the poem "The Cheviot: October"
first appeared, to Stu Ferguson for the use of his excellent grading system
and to Keven Shevels for the use of the photograph on page 9.